SUPER SHOW !
INTERNATIONAL AIR TATTOO & TIGER MEET 1991

by Ian Rentoul, Tom Wakeford & Mark Attrill

CONCORD
PUBLICATIONS COMPANY
CONCORD COLOR SERIES

CONTENTS

INTRODUCTION

Billed as the "World's biggest international air spectacular", The Royal Air Force Benevolent Fund's INTERNATIONAL AIR TATTOO 1991 (IAT 91) took place at RAF Fairford in Oxfordshire, England over the weekend of 20-21 July.

IAT celebrated its 20th anniversary in 1991 and this was the fourth Air Tattoo to the held at RAF Fairford. The two central themes of IAT 91 were the 30th Anniversary Tiger Meet and a Gulf Salute to pay tribute to the airmen and women who played such a vital role in the recent Gulf conflict.

The stage was, therefore, set for what promised to be the premier aviation event in Europe and one of the best Tattoos ever staged. We were not to be disappointed and we were treated to a spectacular eight hour flying display on both days and a static line up of aircraft that stretched for over 2 miles. The mixed weather conditions over the weekend did little to influence the overall outcome of the show - In a word, Superb!.

RAF Fairford, home of the Royal Air Force Benevolent Fund's International Air Tattoo, had seen a considerable change of role since the last IAT in 1989. The United States Air Force had undertaken a gradual withdrawal from the Base during 1990 as US Forces withdrew from Europe following the virtual disbandment of the Warsaw Pact and a thawing of the so-called Cold War. RAF Fairford had been operating as a standby facility since October 1990. When the hostilities in the Gulf commenced in January 1991, RAF Fairford was swiftly reactivated and played a key operational role in the Gulf War when the 806th Bomber Wing with B-52 strategic bombers was assigned to the Base from the Continental United States with the principal task of attacking the Iraqi Republican Guard.

With the Gulf War, and in particular the key art played by air power, still uppermost in most peoples mind it was only right that the Organising Committee should include a special "Gulf Salute". This took the form of a special section which was incorporated in the flying programme on each day, along with a very comprehensive collection of Gulf War participants in the static display. With so many units from the air forces of the United States of America, Great Britain, France, Italy and Canada taking part in Operation DESERT SHIELD/STORM it was perhaps inevitable that we would be treated to a wide range of aircraft types but no-one could have been prepared for the sheer volume of aircraft that IAT 91 had managed to bring together for one weekend in July. It was especially significant that the "Gulf Salute" should take place at RAF Fairford - the only airfield in Europe which launched daily operational missions to the Gulf.

IAT 91 also brought together from around the world, members of the NATO Tiger Association for their five day 30th Anniversary Meet. The last time the Association met at an International Air Tattoo was in 1977, when the show was held at RAF Greenham Common. In the meantime, most of the Tiger Association members had re-equipped and they brought some of the world's most up to date aircraft, many resplendent in a wide variety of colour schemes based on Tiger stripes. Several Tiger Squadrons had also come to RAF Fairford fresh from their exploits in the Gulf War.

The Tiger Squadron Association has members around the world although as a NATO sponsored organisation, most of the participants come from Europe. The first Tiger Meet in 1961 was the result of a request by the French Minister of Defence for a closer relationship and co-operation between the military units of France and the nations of the NATO alliance.

Tiger Meet Dutch style!. Tail markings on one of two Royal Netherlands Air Force F-16A from 313 Sqn.

This year Number 74 (Fighter) Squadron, Royal Air Force, one of the founder members of the Tiger Squadron Association hosted the Tiger Meet. Among those who were at RAF Fairford as first-time visitors were Turkey, with Lockheed F-104 Starfighters, and Portugal with Fiat G-91 "Ginas". The star attraction at Tiger Meet 91 was undoubtedly the appearance of a non-NATO country, Czech and Slovakia which sent two MiG-29 Fulcrums from 11 (Tiger) Regiment based at Zatec. The unit was granted honorary membership to the Tiger Squadron Association and its participation marks the beginning of a new era in east-west relations in the air. Honorary membership has also been extended to include any unit with a "big cat" in its insignia as well as those nations that operate the Northrop F-5E Tiger II. This allowed Switzerland to join in with a pair of F-5Es. Sadly Australia was unable to attend in 1991 so 192 Squadron of the Turkish Air Force should have taken away the Trophy for the crew which travelled the greatest distance to attend.

The Air Tattoo always takes the opportunity to celebrate other notable anniversaries and 1991 was no exception with due recognition to the first flight of the Hawker Hunter in its 40th Anniversary Year. Although the aircraft no longer features in the front-line inventory of the Royal Air Force, and IAT could not boast a line-up as spectacular as that assembled in 1976 to celebrate the 25th anniversary, several interesting UK Ministry of Defence Hunter variants appeared and the Swiss Air Force aerobatic team "Patrouille Suisse" made a welcome return to RAF Fairford.

Another hallmark of the International Air Tattoo is the presence of Europe's finest military aerobatic display teams. We have already mentioned the "Patrouille Suisse" and they were joined this year by the "Patrouille de France", "11 Frecce Tricolori" from Italy, "Team Aguila" from Spain, "The Grasshoppers" from the Netherlands and our very own "Red Arrows". Two civilian teams also participated in IAT 91 - Team ECCO from Dijon in France and the Cadbury's Crunchie Flying Circus from the United Kingdom. "The Falcons" RAF parachute Display Team were also present to thrill the crowds with their skill and precision.

There were so many highlights during International Air Tattoo and Tiger Meet 1991 that it is impossible to single out any one participant or event.

We hope you can sit back and view the images portrayed in this book with as much enjoyment as we had in collecting them together. All of the photographs were taken over a six day period at RAF Fairford by the authors using Canon, Bronica and Olympus camera equipment.

There are many organisations and individuals who assisted us during IAT 91 but in particular we would like to thank the following individuals and organisations for their assistance in making this book possible: First and foremost, The Officer Commanding No. 74 (Fighter) Squadron, Royal Air Force, Wing Commander Graham Clarke; Squadron Leaders Ned Kelly and Martin Loveridge and all other members of the Squadron for their patience and co-operation during IAT and Tiger Meet 91. The Public Relations Staff at the Ministry of Defence (UK) and Headquarters Strike Command, in particular Mr. Michael Hill. The Royal Air Force Benevolent Fund and the IAT Organising Committee for providing such a superb show and press facilities and last but by no means least Mr. Peter R. March for providing us with expert advice on the best photographic locations during the Air Tattoo.

Tail markings on the French Tiger Meet Mirage F.1C. The aircraft, 12-YH was from EC.12 based at Cambrai.

TIGER MEET 1991

Undoubtedly one of the highlights of the Static park. Close -up shot of the Tiger's head on an Italian Air Force F-104 ASA Starfighter. The aircraft belonged to 53 Stormo, one of the units taking part in this year's Tiger Meet.

The Dutch F-16As that took part in Tiger Meet 91 were J-004 and J-012 from 313 Sqn based at Twenthe.

The Dutch take their Tiger Meet markings very seriously and no self respecting F-16 can be seen without Tiger striped wheel chocks!.

Close up view of the tip tank on the stunning Italian Tiger Meet F-104 ASA.

An immaculately presented Mirage F1.C of EC.12 based at Cambrai. The French Air Force obviously take their Tiger Meet markings seriously!

French Air Force F.1C Mirage gets airborne.

French Mirage F.1C 16/12-YH of EC.12 climbs out of RAF Fairford and heads home.

French Air Force CM.170 Magister 572/F-TEAD of Gl.312 based at Salon de Provence.

French Air Force CM.170 Magister from Gl.312 based at Salon de Provence. Note the replacement tip tank, still in its primer paint which spoilt an otherwise immaculate colour scheme.

Colourful Tigers. This view captures the spirit of Tiger Meet 91.

Tiger Meet markings on a Fiat G-91R "Gina" of 301 Squadron, Portuguese Air Force. This fine study amply demonstrates that the G-91 is particularly well suited to the application of Tiger stripes and a cavernous mouth.

A superbly presently Fiat G-91R "Gina" of No. 301 Squadron, Portuguese Air Force. This was the first time the Portuguese had participated in a Tiger Meet and this photograph goes to prove that they have entered into the spirit of the event right from the start.

Close up of the Tiger mouth markings applied to Fiat G-91R 5452 of the Portuguese Air Force.

Tiger stripes on the tail of a Portuguese Fiat G-91T/3 of 301 Squadron.

Fiat G-91T/3 1810 of 301 Squadron, Portuguese Air Force also sported Tiger Meet markings.

CF-18A Hornet 188769 of 439 Squadron, Canadian Armed Force wore this highly effective "low visibility" Tiger Meet colour scheme.

Going Home. CF-18A Hornet of 439 Sqn Canadian Armed Forces taxies towards the runway. The "toned down" Tiger Meet markings were, in reality, very effective.

53rd TFS F-15C Eagle arrives at RAF Fairford for IAT 91.

Tail markings on the 53rd TFS F-15C Eagle celebrating 50 years of the Aircraft Maintenance Unit.

F-15C Eagle of the 53rd TFS based at Bitburg was also sporting a "low visibility" Tiger Meet colour scheme which was particularly well suited to the graceful lines of this large American fighter.

Another United States Air Force Europe Tiger Meet participant was the 79th TFS/20 TFW based at RAF Upper Heyford. Their F-111E 68-049 was sporting full Tiger Meet markings on the tail. The aircraft was also carrying Gulf mission markings.

Tiger's head insignia on the nose of the USAFE F-111E 68-049 from the 79th TFS.

Tail markings on F-111E 68-049. Note the crudely applied serial number.

F-16A FA-94 of 31 Smaldeel, Belgian Air Force in full Tiger Meet markings.

The pilot of the Belgian Air Force F-16A was determined to show off the aircrafts' Tiger Meet markings during departure. The aircraft was from 31 Smaldeel (Squadron) based at Kleine Brogel.

Spanish Air Force EF-18A Hornet which was a Tiger Meet 91 participant.

A Member of the groundcrew checks out this Spanish Air Force EF-18A Hornet. Note the Tiger striped helmet.

During Tiger Meet some participants made every effort to make sure everyone was kitted out with the right gear. The Spanish groundcrew looking after the EF-18 Hornet all wore protective helmets suitably adorned with stripes. On more than one occasion the Dutch crews were caught wearing tiger striped clogs!.

The German Air Force had two units represented at Tiger Meet 91. This RF-4E Phantom 35+26 belongs to AkG 52 at GAF Leck.

The Turkish Air Force made its debut to IAT 91 and Tiger Meet 91 with a pair of F-104Gs from 192 Filo (Squadron). 9-037/63-7037 is seen here landing at the start of the Tattoo.

Tiger Meet tail markings on an Alphajet of the German Air Force. The aircraft is based at Oldenburg with JbG 43.

Close up of the unit insignia applied to the tail surfaces of the Turkish Air Force F-104G 9-037.

Tiger Meet insignia on the fin of the Turkish Air Force TF-104G 65-5911/9-911.

Swiss Air Force F-5E J-3091 lines up for a pairs take-off on the Saturday.

Squadron badge belonging to Staffel 11 of the Swiss Air Force who operate F-5E Tiger II aircraft. A pair of Swiss F-5Es took part in the flying display on both days.

Checks complete. One of the two Swiss Air Force F-5E display pilots dismounts..........

.... I couldn't understand what they said but they appeared happy with their performance!.

Aero L-39ZA Albatross 2436 of the Czech and Slovak Air Force with the display pilot somewhat reluctantly posing by the cockpit.

Close up of the Albatross insignia on the air intake of the Czech L-39ZA.

Aero L-39ZA Albatross 2436 of 1 Squadron/11 Wing. This aircraft carried a Tiger striped fin band and Unit insignia for Tiger Meet 91.

A wave from the pilot of this Czech Aero L-39ZA Albatross as he taxies out to commence his air display.

Czech and Slovak Air Force Mig 29 7501 of 1 Squadron/11 Wing has probably become one of the first East European victims of the "Zapping" disease!. That's what happens when you take part in Tiger Meet!.

MiG 29 7501 of 1 Squadron/11 Wing participated in Tiger Meet and the IAT 91 flying programme. The aircraft carried a Tiger striped fin band and a crow insignia on the inner fin surfaces. The Squadron badge which incorporates a leaping Tiger is carried on the side of the air intakes. In this view, the aircraft is seen arriving at IAT 91 with 5616 which appeared in the static park.

Czech Mig 29 "7501" on the operational dispersal. Note the tiger striped fin top and the crow marking on the inner fin surfaces.

MiG 29 "Fulcrum" of the Czech and Slovak Air Force at rest.

Close up of the 1 Squadron badge on the intake.

Close up of the crow insignia on the inner fin surfaces.

No. 230 Squadron, Royal Air Force presented some of the most attractive and striking markings of Tiger Meet 91 with their Puma HC.1 XW224/DH.

Considerable time and effort had gone into the production of the intricate Tigers head emblazoned on the fuselage of Puma HC.1 XW224.

Tiger's head on the nose of a Sea King HAS.6 from 814 Naval Air Squadron of the Royal Navy which took part in Tiger Meet 91.

Close up shot of the 230 Squadron insignia applied to the nose of the Tiger Meet Puma.

Tornado GR.1A ZG726/K of 13 Squadron was one of three RAF aircraft that displayed Tiger Meet markings.

Close up shot of the Tiger's head marking applied to the 13 Sqn Tornado GR.1A.

A fine study of Phantom FGR.2 XV415/0 of 74 (Fighter) Squadron. The Squadron is one of the three founder members of the Tiger Association which celebrated its 30th anniversary with Tiger Meet 91.

The host unit, No. 74 Squadron, Royal Air Force provided a Phantom FGR.2 with special tail markings. The finish on the aircraft was immaculate and it was by far cleanest example of this McDonnel Douglas fighter ever seen by the photographer, outside of a Museum!.

Close up shot of the tail markings applied to XV423/Y of 74 Squadron. Sadly, the markings applied to the host units aircraft were far less flamboyant than those originally proposed.

Aircrew and Groundcrew perform last minute checks on the Phantom FRG.2s of 74 Squadron prior to their participation in the afternoons flying programme.

74 (Fighter) Squadron Commander, Wing Commander Graham Clarke.

Close up study of a 74 Squadron Phantom cockpit. Note the nose markings which incorporate a Tiger's head flanked by Tiger stripes. Another Tiger's head appears in a white circle on the fin along with more Tiger stripes on the RWR fairing.

The four Phantom FGR.2s from 74 Squadron in formation. The Squadron worked extremely hard to perfect an imaginative display and benefitted from the experience of several ex-Red Arrows team members.

Phantom FGR.2 XT914/Z holds on the runway immediately prior to take-off.

The 74 Squadron formation display impressed the crowd at the International Air Tattoo.

A fine air to air study of a Phantom FGR.2 of No. 74 (Fighter) Squadron.

A 74 (Fighter) Squadron formates for the benefit of the photographer.

A 74 Sqn Phantom FGR.2 takes the drogue for a quick top up.

Tiger Mania!. This Ford Transit did not escape the attentions of one Tiger Meet Squadron.

Phantom FGR.2 XT905/P comes in to land on completion of the formation display.

FAST JETS

French Air Force Mirage F1.C from EC.12 makes a smart take off.

Super Etendard Number 65 of 17 Flotille, French Navy taxies across the threshold to become one of the attractions in the south side static display park.

Super Etendard of 17 Flotille, French Navy performs a slow fly-by with everything down.

The clean lines of the Super Etendard can be seen in this fine study.

French Navy Super Etendard taxies down the runway with its brake chute deployed on completion of a fine air display.

The French Air Force sent two Mirage 2000Bs to IAT 91. Here 512/2-FI of EC. 2/2 makes for an impressive departure prior to display in the flying programme.

Mirage 2000B made a noisy departure on the Monday!

French Air Force Mirage 2000B from Mont-de-Marsan was one of two that took part in Tiger Meet 91 and the IAT 91 flying programme. The 2000B is a trainer aircraft with full operational capability.

Alphajet Es of the French Air Force display team, the Patrouille de France bask in the sunshine. The team made its UK debut with the type ten years earlier at IAT 81.

EF-18 of the Spanish Air Force taxies back to its' dispersal after a spirited flying display on the Sunday.

This Spanish Air Force Mirage F.1CE was one of two that took part in Tiger Meet 91. The aircraft is wearing a recently revised "low vis" scheme.

The Spanish Air Force aerobatic display team "Team Aguila".

"Team Aguila" arriving at RAF Fairford for IAT 91.

"Team Aguila" head towards the crowd line.

"Team Aguila" fly the CASA 101 Aviojet trainer aircraft. The team made its debut at IAT in 1987.

Three Hunter F.58s of the "Patrouille Suisse" take off in formation prior to commencing their display routine.

A Hunter F.58 of the Patrouille Suisse comes in to land following an impressive display of formation aerobatics. This particular aircraft wears a special red and white scheme on the undersurfaces to celebrate the 700 anniversary of the foundation of Switzerland. The Swiss Air Force has been a major user of the Hawker Hunter for the past three decades.

The distinctive underside markings applied to several Hunters of the "Patrouille Suisse" can be seen in this view.

The "Patrouille Suisse" line up on the ORP prior to moving out for a formation take off.

Dutch two seat F-16B J-656 from 311 Squadron on departure.

One of two Dutch F-16s that appeared in special anniversary markings. The Royal Netherlands Air Force had no less than nine F-16s in attendance at IAT 91.

F-16B crew. Note the Tiger striped helmets!.

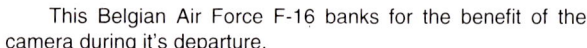

This Belgian Air Force F-16 banks for the benefit of the camera during it's departure.

Belgian Air Force F-16A comes in to land.

Regular visitors to IAT are 16 Smaldeel (Squadron) from the Belgian Air Force. This time they sent BD-03, a Mirage 5BD two place operational trainer.

The Belgian Air Force Alphajet that was displayed so well by Commandant Dany Payeur.

The attractive colour scheme applied to the Belgian Air Force Alphajet shows up well in this fine shot.

Commandant Dany Payeur takes off to begin his display with the Belgian Air Force Alphajet. This is Commandant Payeur's second season as the Alphajet demonstration pilot.

Belgian Air Force Alphajet AT-12.

The crew of this Turkish Air Force TF-104G wait patiently for their turn to leave during the departure's day, This was the first International Air Tattoo attended by the Turkish Air Force. Number 192 Filo (Squadron) is home based at Balikesir.

A welcome visitor to IAT 91 was this A-7P Corsair II of The Portuguese Air Force.

Portuguese TA-7P Corsair II 5549 from 304 Squadron begins its' take off run.

The Portuguese Air Force sent a sizeable contingent to IAT 91 including a pair of T-38s from 103 Squadron.

A T-38A of the Portuguese Air Force in an attractive white colour scheme which highlights the aircraft's sleek shape.

The crew of this Canadian CF-18B appear relaxed as they head for home.

Canadian Armed Forces CF-18A of 439 Squadron from Baden-Sollingen in Germany. Note that the wings have yet to extend fully.

A German Navy Tornado of Mfg 1 makes a clean getaway early on the Monday morning.

One of two German Air Force F-4F Phantoms from JG 71. The two aircraft sported different variations of the current low-visibility colour scheme applied to German Air Defence aircraft.

Italian Air Force Tornado of the 36 Stormo, resplendent in the Gulf colour scheme.

This Italian Air Force Tornado, caught by the camera lens on departure, carries the markings of the 36 Stormo. The large number on the rudder is not a regular marking; it was applied for the recent Paris Air Show.

Tiger's head insignia on the intake of an Italian Air Force Tornado.

A Tornado of the Italian Air Force starts its long journey home. This aircraft (50-36) was the lone example from the 50 Stormo.

Another aircraft making its debut at IAT 91 was this AMX Ground Attack fighter of 51 Stormo. 51 Stormo previously operated F-104 Starfighters.

Italian Air Force AMX Fighter RS-14 from the RSV shows off the neat lines of this small, agile fighter bomber.

FRECCE TRICOLORI arrive at RAF Fairford.

Three MB.339As of the Italian Frecce Tricolori line up for a breathtaking formation takeoff performed by the entire team!.

The attractive colour scheme worn by the FRECCE TRICOLORI can be seen to advantage in this nice shot of a singleton aircraft.

The Italian Air Force aerobatic display team FRECCE TRICOLORI always put on an impressive display and IAT 91 was no exception. They seem to have recovered well from the tragedy that befell them at Ramstein some years ago.

The arrival of this Czech MiG 23ML caused a lot of excitement. This was the first time a Mig 23 had visited the United Kingdom and the aircraft formed part of the large contingent form Czechoslovakia.

Czech and Slovak MiG 23ML at rest in the static park.

The Czech MiG 23 sported a large Squadron badge on the nose. The devils Trident failed to ward off the attention of several Squadron Zappers including the Patrouille Suisse!.

Czech MiG 23L 4644 lights the 'burner on departure at the end of IAT 91.

Welcome visitors at IAT 91 were two A-7D Corsair IIs of the 112th Tactical Fighter Group/Pennsylvania Air National Guard, including 73-997 which is shown here. The A-7s were accompanied by a KC-135E for their long flight from the United States.

F-4G "Wild Weasel" of the 52nd TFW based at Spagdahlen in Germany.

Phantom F-4G 69-7212 of the 52nd TFW departs from RAF Fairford, This particular aircraft was a veteran of the Gulf War and formed part of IAT 91's "Gulf Salute" in the static park.

Strike mission markings on a USAFE F-4G indicate that this particular aircraft took part in Operation Desert Storm.

SAM killer double act. This F-4G "Wild Weasel" and F-16C are part of the Air Wing based at Spangdahlen in Germany which specialises in the destruction of Surface to Air Missile sites. Their success in this mission was ably proven during the Gulf War.

This F-16C from Ramstein Air Base in Germany arrived at Fairford with a full complement of AIM-9 missiles.

United States Air Force Europe F-16C of the 526th TFS, 86th TFW based at Ramstein takes off to formate with a colleague during IAT's "Gulf Salute" flying programme.

F-16C 85-422/RS from the 526th TFS seen departing from RAF Fairford. The aircraft earlier took part in the "Gulf Salute" flying programme. Note the addition of a ferry pod on the outer underwing pylon.

Spagdahlen based F-16C from the 52nd TFW complete with a very effective sharksmouth. Some enthusiasts have always wondered why the F-16 was not named the "Shark" since its sleek grey lines and cavernous "mouth" give it an appearance more akin to the marine predator than a bird of prey.

Special Tail Markings on a F-16C Fighting Falcon. The aircraft belongs to the 612th Tactical Fighter Squadron based at Torrejon in Spain.

A pair of F-15Cs from the 57th FIS, based at Keflavik, Iceland depart from Fairford.

The USAFE 36th Tactical Fighter Wing at Bitburg, Germany sent 4 Eagles to IAT 91 including F-15C 80-022/BT which took part in the flying programme. This particular aircraft had special tail markings for the 22nd TFS.

This F-15C (84-019) from Bitburg's 53rd TFS displays two Iraqi kill markings under the cockpit.

F-15C 80-022/BT from the 36th TFW at Bitburg, Germany. The air defence grey scheme shows up well against the storm clouds looming in the background.

F-15C from the 36th TFW Bitburg, makes an impressive departure from Fairford's runway.

This Jaguar GR.1A belongs to Number 54 Squadron, one of three RAF Squadrons based at RAF Coltishall in Norfolk that still operate the Jaguar. The primary role of the aircraft is Ground Attack and Tactical Reconnaissance. This particular aircraft is wearing a special colour scheme applied to celebrate the 75th Anniversary of 54 (F) Sqn.

Tail markings on Jaguar GR.1A XZ112/GA of 54 Squadron.

Taking part in the "Gulf Salute" was this veteran of the Gulf War, Jaguar GR.1A XZ356/EP. The aircraft actually belongs to 6 Squadron but was operated by Number 41 (composite) Squadron during the conflict.

Jaguar GR.1A XZ356/EP resplendent in Gulf War colour scheme and carrying a representative warload.

Buccaneer S2B XX885/L is in fact nicknamed "Caroline" and carried appropriate nose art on the starboard side along with the obligatory name of a whisky. All of the RAF's operational Buccaneers are now based at RAF Lossiemouth in Scotland. They are due to be replaced by Tornados within the next two years.

Jolly Roger nose art on Buccaneer S2B XX885/L which was in the static park and formed part of the "Gulf Salute". Each of the Buccs' that deployed to the Gulf sported a Jolly Roger all of which were of a slightly different design.

The Buccaneer still makes an impressive sight on take off. Sadly the type does not feature much in flying programmes these days.

Tornado GR.1 ZA465/FK "Foxy Killer" made a welcome appearance in the static park. There were three RAF Tornados in the Gulf colour scheme at RAF Fairford.

Tornado GR.1 ZA410/EX in Gulf War colour scheme gives the crowd some idea of the view from a former Iraqi Air Force Base Commander's office window!.

Tornado GR.1 ZA465/FK "Foxy Killer" of No. 16 Squadron, Royal Air Force departs RAF Fairford. The aircraft carries the markings it wore during Operation Granby and a typical warload.

75th Anniversary scheme on a Royal Air Force Tornado GR.1 of 45 Squadron/Tornado Weapons Conversion Unit, based at RAF Honington.

This Tornado GR.1 was one of two from No.45 (Shadow) Squadron/Tornado Weapons Conversion Unit which carried special anniversary markings. Both sets of markings were different and celebrated the anniversaries of both parts of this composite unit.

Variation on a theme. Yet another 75th Anniversary scheme from the Tornado Weapons Conversion Unit/45 Squadron.

Fast, Low and extremely noisy! Tornado GR.1 ZA609/J of 617 (Dambuster) Squadron departs RAF Fairford with the aid of the afterburners.

Tornado F.3 display crew about to leave the dispersal in the "spare" aircraft. The Tornado F.3 display crew for 1991 are Flt Lt Archie Neill (Pilot) and Flt Lt Jim Brown (Navigator).

Tornado F.3 ZE969/EA of 23 Squadron leaves RAF Fairford in murky weather.

The RAF Tornado F.3 display aircraft for 1991 is drawn from No.25 (Fighter) Squadron based at RAF Leeming in Yorkshire. ZE167, seen here displaying its short landing performance, has been painted in a special black, silver and light grey display scheme.

RAF Tornado F.3 being put through its paces on the second day of IAT 91.

Royal Air Force Tornado F.3 of 25 Squadron, based at RAF Leeming. This aircraft is in a special 1991 airshow colour scheme as the Squadron celebrated their 75th Anniversary in 1990.

Royal Air Force Tornado F.3 ZE808/FA of 25 Squadron gets airborne for its flying display.

Hawker Hunter T.7B WV318 of 237 OCU in a special all black scheme to celebrate the 40th birthday of Sir Sydney Camm's classic jet fighter design. 237 OCU is in fact the Buccaneer Operational Conversion Unit but as no Buccaneer trainer exists the Hunter is used for the initial operational training of Buccaneer crews. The black colour scheme was based on that used by the "Black Arrows", the 111 Squadron aerobatic display team who performed at many airshows during the early sixties.

Tornado F.3 ZE761/CB of No. 5 Squadron arrives in overcast conditions at RAF Fairford.

This Harrier T4 of No. 233 Operational Conversion Unit was an unexpected surprise on the Monday when it arrived from RAF Wittering to deliver a ferry pilot for one of the static display aircraft.

This Hawk T.1 and Hunter GA.11 combination appeared on several occasions during the arrivals day but did not stay for the Tattoo. The Hawk was from RAF Valley and the Hunter belongs to the Fleet Requirements and Direction Unit (FRADU) at RNAS Yeovilton.

Hawk T.1 of 4 Flying Training School, Royal Air Force holds at the threshold prior to final clearance for take-off.

Hawk T.1A on arrivals day. Note the AIM.9 Sidewinder fit.

Hawk T.1 XX249 of No. 4 Flying Training School, RAF Valley tucks up its undercarriage on departure.

BAe Hawk T.1 of No. 4 Flying Training Squadron, RAF Valley. The aircraft wears a special scheme to celebrate the 75th Anniversary of the School.

Tail markings on Hawk T.1A XX289 of No. 63 Squadron, 2TWU based at RAF Chivenor.

Tail markings on Hawk T.1A of No. 2 Tactical Weapons Unit based at RAF Chivenor in Devon.

Smoke on Go! The Royal Air Force Aerobatic Display Team, the Red Arrows depart for their home at RAF Scampton on the Monday following the show.

75th anniversary scheme on Phantom FGR.2 XV408/Z of 92 Squadron.

Tail Marking on Phantom FGR.2 XT899/B of 19 Sqn.

Tail Markings on Phantom FGR.2 XV408/Z. This aircraft belongs to 92 Squadron who resided with 19 Squadron at RAF Wildenrath in Germany.

The two Phantoms from 19 and 92 Squadron depart for RAF Wildenrath at the end of IAT 91.

75th anniversary scheme on Phantom FGR.2 XT899/B of 19 (Fighter) Squadron which recently disbanded at RAF Wildenrath in Germany.

Phantom FGR.2 XV408/Z 92 (India) Squadron, Royal Air Force comes in to land. This historic Squadron is one of those affected by the partial withdrawal of the RAF withdrawal from Germany, and will disband later this year.

A legacy of reunification. The "new" German Air Force has inherited several Antonov AN-24 transport aircraft from the former East German Air Force and has pressed them into service on short haul routes. AN-24 52+07 Transport Squadron 24 made several visits prior to the show before entering the static park on the Friday.

The propellors of this Italian Air Force Fiat G.222 whip up the condensation in the air as it winds up its engines for the long journey home. This particular aircraft was not actually part of IAT 91, but delivered support personnel and equipment to RAF Fairford on the Thursday preceeding the show.

Boeing 707-338C A20-627 of No.33 Squadron, Royal Australian Air Force. Note the presence of flight refuelling pods on the outer wing. The RAAF have converted the Boeings so that they now have a limited, point refuelling capability, similar to the system being fitted to RAF VC10 C.1 transport aircraft of No. 10 Sqn.

Considerable interest was generated by the arrival of this Antonov AN-12 of the Czech and Slovak Air Force.

Antonov AN-12 2105 of No.1 Dopravni Squadron on arrival at RAF Fairford.

A wave from the crew of the Czech AN-12 as they head for home.

Antonov AN-12 of the Czech and Slovak Air Force brought most of the support equipment required by the Czech detachment. Rumour has it that the aircraft went back with considerably more after the Czechs experienced a Free Market economy!.

One of the workhorses of Military Airlift Command. The C-141B Starlifter, another familiar sight at RAF Fairford, gave sterling service during Operation Desert Shield, the build-up of US Forces in the Gulf.

One of the undisputed stars of this year's IAT was the Tupolev TU-134A of the Czech and Slovak Air Force. Although the aircraft stayed in the static park over the weekend it was called upon to return home on Sunday evening to pick up spare parts for a MiG 29 that became unserviceable during the flying programme.

Another rare visitor to the UK and to IAT was this E-3C of the 965th AWCS, United States Air Force.

KC-10A 30075 of the 2nd BW on arrival at Fairford. Many were pleased to see that the USAF had thoughtfully provided an aircraft in the more aesthetically pleasing "SAC" colour scheme.

A KC-135E of the Pennsylvania Air National Guard arrives on familiar territory. RAF Fairford was once the largest base in Europe for USAF flight refuelling operations and KC-135s were familiar sights in the skies above the Oxfordshire base.

This KC-135E of the 147th ARS/Pennsylvania Air National Guard accompanied a pair of A-7s from the same Guard unit to IAT 91. The aircraft took part in air operations during the Gulf War and sported nose art special markings to celebrate this achievement.

The USAF E-3 AWACS revealed several Gulf mission markings on the nose.

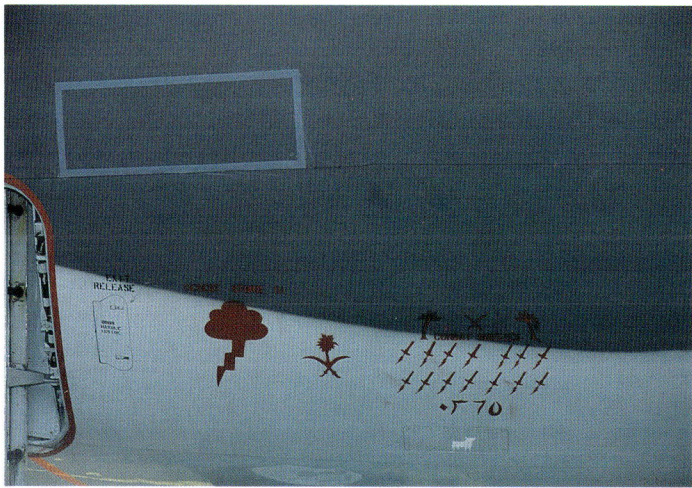

A plethora of mission symbols and markings stencilled onto the nose of a USAF KC-135 indicated its involvement in Gulf War air operations.

A-10A 79-218/WR caught in the afternoon sun at IAT 91.

A-10A 79-218WR of the 92nd TFS based at RAF Woodbridge in East Anglia displays a plethora of mission markings following action during the Gulf conflict.

A-10As at rest. Two Thunderbolts from the 92nd TFS at RAF Woodbridge took part in the flying programme.

One of two Lakenheath based F-111Fs from the 492nd TFS/48 TFW that attended IAT 91 departs from RAF Fairford.

This F-111 was one of several such machines in the static park displaying mission markings from Operation Desert Storm.

F-111E 68-029/UH of the 55th TFS/20 TFW was one of three Aardvarks from "down the road" at RAF Upper Heyford.

MC-130E Hercules in the Sunday afternoon sunshine.

Boeing B-52G 80229 of the 97th BW was one of two "Buffs" at IAT 91. The aircraft in the static park was a B-52H.

B-52G 80229 deploys its 'chute on landing at RAF Fairford. The "Buff" became a familiar sight over Oxfordshire during February 1991 when it once again returned to RAF Fairford to take part in the air war against Iraq.

Nose art on B-52G 80229 of the 97th BW. This aircraft, nicknamed "Sioux Warrior" took park in the "Gulf Salute" flying programme.

"Sioux Warrior" taxies back to the dispersal after its flying display. The routine must have been hot work judging by the open window!.

Nose Art on B-52H 00031 of the 7th Bomber Wing.

Boeing pair. Two very different types from the same stable are captured in this shot. A B-52G backtracks down the runway as a Boeing 707 Freighter of Anglo Cargo Airlines flies overhead.

The controversial B-1B Bomber made another welcome appearance at IAT 91. It may not work as advertised but it is still a very good looking piece of heavy metal! This particular example is 60140 from the 384th Bomber Wing.

BAe Nimrod MR.2P XV233 of 42 Squadron, RAF comes in to land at RAF Fairford.

BAe Nimrod MR.2P of 42 (Torpedo Bomber) Squadron, Royal Air Force made a spectacular take off on the Sunday. The Nimrod is used for Maritime Patrol, Surveillance and Anti-Submarine duties and is based on the old Comet airliner design.

BAe Nimrod MR.2P "crewing up" prior to its air display in the flying programme.

Close up of the special tail markings applied to XV233 to celebrate the 75th anniversary of No.42 (Torpedo Bomber)

The mighty Vulcan bomber taxies out to begin its traditional display which never fails to impress the crowd. We sincerely hope that this will not be the last airshow season for this classic bomber which has become a piece of Britains' aviation heritage.

Royal Air Force Sentry AEW.1 ZH102 of the recently re-equipped 8 Squadron made a welcome debut at IAT 91. The Sentry aircraft, based on the Boeing E-3A AWACS aircraft, is the most recent addition to the Royal Air Force inventory and replaced the Shackleton Airborne Early Warning aircraft.

Avro Vulcan B.2 XH558 of the Vulcan Display Flight at rest.

Newest aircraft in the Royal Air Force inventory is the Boeing E-3 Sentry AEW.1 which was ordered when the Nimrod AEW programme was terminated in the early eighties.

Tristar K.1 ZD951 of 216 Squadron, Royal Air Force on take off. ZD951 was one of two Tristars painted in Desert Pink during the Gulf War and was nicknamed the "Pink Pig".

A rather weary looking VC.10 K.2 Tanker of 101 Squadron, Royal Air Force comes in to land. This aircraft type played an important role in the recent Gulf War. All nine VC.10 tankers of 101 Sqn were based in Saudi Arabia during the conflict, refuelling RAF and Coalition aircraft on missions to and from Iraq.

Air to air study of Tristar K.1 ZD951 of 216 Squadron, Royal Air Force. Nicknamed the "Pink Pig", this Tristar was one of two such aircraft that played a key role in providing air to air refuelling alongside VC10 and Victor aircraft of the RAF's Tanker Force.

ROTARY WINGS

Alouette III H-20 of the Royal Netherlands Air Force SAR Flight.

Bell UH-1D 71+02 Ltg 64, German Air Force.

Bell UH-1H 69-15605 of Headquarters US Army Command Europe.

Puma HC.1 XW220/CZ of 33 Squadron based at RAF Odiham in Hampshire. The aircraft wears the colour scheme applied for operations in the Gulf. Note the presence of the Squadron insignia in black on the cockpit door. This marking was not carried during the Gulf War which suggests that the aircraft has had a respray since its return from Saudi Arabia.

Sea King HC.4 ZG829 of the Empire Test Pilots School was on hand over the weekend to provide air support for the fire fighting services.

Wessex HC.2 XS679/WG of No. 2 Flying Training School from RAF Shawbury. 2 FTS provides all the initial training for those pilots destined to fly helicopters in the Royal Air Force.

Puma HC.1 XW226 of 230 Squadron, currently based at RAF Gutersloh in Germany but due to move to RAF Laarbruch during 1992.

Wessex HC.2 XR518 of 22 Squadron, RAF Chivenor, which gave an impressive air display on both days of the show.

POT POURRI

This colourful Canberra B2 belongs to the German Air Force.

Another rare and unexpected visitor to IAT 91 was this Dornier 28 Skyservant.

The bright orange coloured Canberra B2s of the German Air Force are familiar sights at International Air Tattoo.

Germany was one of three NATO countries that sent Atlantic Maritime Patrol Aircraft to IAT 91. This example is operated by Mfg3 of the German Navy.

Close up of a Breguet Atlantique 2 from the French Navy. There was a good representation of NATO Anti- Submarine and Maritime Patrol aircraft at IAT 91.

Breguet Atlantique 2 belonging to the French Navy. The open weapons bay and deployed ASW radar can be clearly seen in this view.

A Breguet Atlantique 2 of the French Navy was another interesting visitor to IAT 91.

Atlantique 2 of the French Navy.

This French Air Force CM.170 Magister primary jet trainer was one of five such aircraft that visited IAT 91, including one in very attractive Tiger Meet markings.

The tail of a BAC 1-11 belonging to No. 4 Squadron of the Sultan of Oman's Air Force.

The French Air Force sent a C-160NG Transall to IAT 91, principally in support of the Patrouille de France aerobatic display team.

Royal Netherlands Navy P-3C 301 of 320 Squadron took part in a flying programme packed with variety.

The Royal Netherlands Navy is a relative newcomer to the P-3C Orion. This Lockheed design replaced the long serving SP-2H Neptunes of 320 Squadron at Valkenburg in the early eighties.

P-3C Orion 301 of No.320 Sqn, Royal Netherlands Navy.

Royal Netherlands Air Force F-27 Troopship. Sadly this aircraft did not appear in this year's flying programme. Many IAT fans will remember the amazing performances of previous shows with an ex-fighter pilot at the controls of this surprisingly agile transport aircraft.

The P-3C Orion family of Maritime Patrol Aircraft made a significant contribution to IAT 91. This particular aircraft is in fact a CP-140 Aurora of 415 Squadron, Canadian Armed Forces.

This Casa CN235 of the Spanish Air Force sports a rather distinctive camouflage scheme which appears to be catering for all the natural environments the aircraft may find itself operating in !.

The long distance visitor prize must almost certainly have gone to the crew of this Royal Australian Air Force C-130E Hercules of No.37 Squadron. The RAAF Air Transport Force are regular visitors to the International Air Tattoo.

EC-130E 637869 of the 193rd Special Operations Squadron/ Pennsylvania Air National Guard was one of nine C-130 variants brought by the United States Forces to IAT 91.

High visibility! Enthusiasts had few problems visually acquiring this Civilian Learjet from Switzerland. It is understood that the aircraft was used to ferry maintenance personnel and spares from and to Switzerland. The Swiss Air Force does not possess its own Air Transport assets.

MC-130 Hercules of the 7th SOS based at Rhein-Main AB in Germany basks in the afternoon sun.

Closer inspection of a US C-130 Hercules revealed its participation in Operation "Provide Comfort", the relief operation that was set up to aid the Kurdish refugees in the aftermath of the Gulf War.

Nose art on KC-135Q 80046 "Black Sheep" of the 380th Bomber Wing.

The 42nd ECS equipped with EF-111As shares Upper Heyford with the F-111s of the 20 TFW. The EF-111A Electronic Counter Measures aircraft from Upper Heyford were used with great effect during Operation Desert Storm.

This EP-3E Aries of VQ-2, United States Navy is a very rare visitor to Britain. The aircraft is based on the P-3 Orion Maritime Patrol and Anti-Submarine aircraft, also used by the USN.

Some colour on a TR-1A. Seeing is believing!. This interesting character was caught on the tail of an example from the 95th Reconnaissance Squadron.

A P-3C Orion of the United Stated Navy. Many enthusiasts have lamented the US Navy's decision to do away with individual Squadron markings on the tail surfaces which became one of the hallmarks of the Orion fleet.

EC-135H 10282 of the 10th ACCS, United States Air Force Europe.

A rather special and very rare visitor to IAT 91 was this EA-3B of VQ-2 based at Naval Air Station Rota in Spain. The almost obligatory USN sharksmouth is evident in this view!.

Overall view of the EA-3B, affectionately known as the "Whale". This will probably be the last time this type is seen at an airshow in the UK.

This close up shot of the rear fuselage of the EA-3B Skywarrior from VQ-2 reveals a Gulf War mission marking. The specific mission of the EA-3B is a closely guarded secret even as it reaches retirement age.

EA-3B Skywarrior of VQ-2, United States Navy burns some rubber on landing. Note the "Sandeman" figure on the fin based on a famous Sherry brand label.

This Buccaneer S.2B is operated by the Ministry of Defence at the Aircraft & Armament Experimental Establishment, Boscombe Down in Wiltshire. The special paint scheme is used in connection with trails work on the aircraft.

BAe 125 CC.3 of 32 Squadron, Royal Air Force. The aircraft is sporting a rather smart "low-visibility" colour scheme which differs somewhat from the normal business jet image!. Note the ECM fairing on the extreme tail just below the rudder.

Jet Provost T.5A XW427/67 of No.1 Flying Training School. The Jet Provost is nearing the end of its service life and is being gradually replaced by the Shorts Tucano T.1.

This Jet Provost T.5B belongs to No.6 Flying Training Squadron. It is one of two aircraft with a special display colour scheme first seen in 1990.

Spitfire VB AB910/MD-E of the Battle of Britain Memorial Flight makes a high speed pass over RAF Fairford. The BBMF is based at RAF Coningsby in Lincolnshire.

A familiar sight at airshows around the United Kingdom. The Lancaster B.Mk1 of the Battle of Britain Memorial Flight taxies out to take part in the flying programme.

This year's aerobatic team participation included one civilian team, sponsored by Martini and flying the Pilatus PC-9 trainer aircraft. The team put on an impressive display of formation aerobatics during Saturday's flying programme.

Shorts Tucano T.1 ZF245 of the Royal Air Force with the "Grasshoppers" aerobatic display team of the Royal Netherlands Air Force in the background.

A flare is lit in front of the VIP enclosure to indicate the start of a display by RAF "Falcons" Parachute Display Team based at RAF Brize Norton........... And here they come!

Unsung heroes. We should not forget the massive participation by the emergency services who came from far and wide and included RAF, British Army, USAF, US Army, and civilian fire and medical services, Military and civilian police agencies, and voluntary first aid institutions amongst others.

The US Air Force provided a large contingent of fire fighting vehicles for IAT 91.

Some of the many emergency service vehicles that were present at RAF Fairford for IAT 91. This particular contingent is from the Royal Air Force. Thankfully their services were not required during the accident-free week of flying.

COALITION AIRPOWER IN DESERT STORM

4022 F-15E Strike Eagle & F-15C Eagle
'Target Baghdad!'

9903 Tornado GR.1
'Mig Eater'

4516 A-6E TRAM Intruder
'VA-85 Black Falcons'

4526 AV-8B Night Attack Harrier
'VX-5 Vampires'

4529 F-14A Plus Tomcat
'VF-101 Grim Reapers'

4020 F-14A w/deck vehicles
'Launch!'

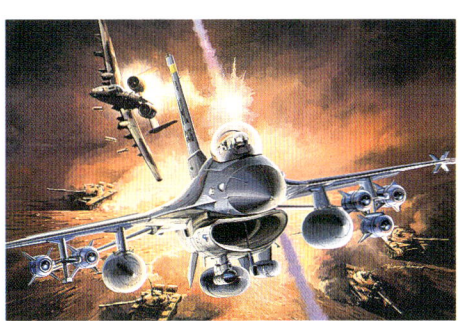

4535 F-16C Night Falcon

4530 AH-64B Longbow Apache

4534 F-15E Dual-Role Fighter

4536 F-18D Hornet

"STEPS AHEAD .....ALWAYS!"

OUR DESERT STORM SERIES

4001 BLITZKRIEG IN THE GULF

2002 OPERATION GRANBY

2003 OPERATION DESERT SHIELD

2004 U.S. AIRPOWER IN DESERT STORM

2005 GULF WAR:BRITISH AIR ARMS

CONCORD PUBLICATIONS COMPANY

2006 OPERATION DESERT SABRE